SHADOW TRUTHS

SHADOW TRUTHS

poems

V. RENDINA

atmosphere press

Contents

too much! too much!

too

adverb

    1. to a higher degree than is permissible, or possible;
          excessively

they say you can never have

too much

of a good thing but that goes
against the mere definition
already there's too much
more than allowed
more than you should take

i'm a huge fan of coffee and
i'm never happy with just one
single cup some days i need
two or three some days my
day's not complete until i've
had that late night eighth

too much.

i drink too much and smoke too much
hell i shower too much when the mood's right

will there ever be enough for me?
or am i constantly set out to see
what truly lies at the bottom of
a bottle, inside the grinds of my
coffee cup. will i find enough

through a morning message meant for

sleepy eyes to swallow without
cream and sugar, black and bitter
or will you set it aside to go cold
because you've had your fill

you say you can never have

too much

of me but that goes
against every last breath or silent
sigh i over-poured for you, and
you said you didn't mean it
but you said i'm not enough
so which one is it?

will i ever be enough for you?
have i reached the point of
permission, am i being
unreasonable, over and
over and over again
because my fill falls above
your limit should i really
drink this much?

i feel too much
i love too much

is too much of too much a bad thing?
i forget too often not everyone can
have too much; sometimes they
settle with the quiet comfort of

enough

stuck on the rim of their cup
after the first lonely swig
some people know when they've had

too much and you promised you could
take it all but i never know when to stop

too

adverb

2.   in addition; also

synonyms: also, as well

well, have i given you too much
of a good thing? and in addition
is it enough to admit
i can't get enough

of coffee?
of booze, smooth jazz, and hard rock?
of sex and drugs and cheap perfume?
of anything regarding you?

you.

i can never get too much of you
and not as another additive in
my insatiable sense of what i need
my addictive personality comes out
with you, i never know if i'm
enough for you, when i feel
too much and you promised you
would take it all but will it be

too much

for you when it's never
enough for me?

i crave you

before my morning cigarette with a
cup of coffee, i'm still searching for
that caffeine buzz i taste when we
kiss, your lips subtle and soft, you
wake me better than that sixth shot
of espresso requested in my drink

kissing you tastes of live wire pressed
firm against my lips, and every hot jolt
screams "too much! too much!"

too much

is that good or bad?
is chasing you another lonely night
bar crawl chasing jameson with
a second shot of hard liquor
or are you the water that eases
the burn and softens the pain

too

adverb

   3. moreover

i still can't seem to get my fill
still searching for an angry fix off
too many words that mean nothing
and everything, too many sounds
meant only to sound suitable
when spoken out loud

but you sound good to me
(would it be too much to
say that out loud?) i beg for
more than just one quick hit
and you promised you can

take it all but i can't quite figure out
if that's too much for me or just

enough

a (rise and) fall of stardust

you are the warmth against the cool sting
of a summer rain. Fools stuck between time and
Timbuktu and the unpredictable nature of another
midnight storm.

we looked up to the night sky, water spot
stars glint on smudged glasses under the
streetlight glow

like stargazing

I claimed

with galaxies formed before my eyes
the drizzle unfolding into meteor showers

stars splayed out in puddles against the
nothing
and
everything

consuming us

your hand slips into mine as Halley's Comet soars between
Mercury and Venus (or two unaccountable freaks)
and over the bridge of my nose.

like stargazing

You agree

and I shift my focus back into orbit
while stardust glimmers all around you.

June, 1889

we pay our respects to the dead
in museums erected under the
weight of their life. i summon
myself to your work, a Wake
in mourning of your Starry Night.
i saw you once from a blurry
distance, ablaze in muted blues
with shades of hope in every subtle
brush stroke

they say you would
eat your yellow paint to
put your mind at ease with all
that sadness spilled upon the
canvas. your misery for the
world to see, yet no one seems to
see your sorrow

while you hang there

crowds cluster around you,
cramped and crouched
searching for the perfect
angle, the right lighting, an
inconsistent metaphor

(i'd have brought you
sunflowers if i could)

cameras suffocate you,
dizzy curls under harsh
flashes framed besides a
plaque shouting unwanted
fame in

MoMA gothic typeface
Dutch, 1853-1890

An Unexpected
Masterpiece
Oil on canvas

do all these sad eyes make
you nervous?

i'm shaking
in your presence

you painted strokes of
sorrow, bloody wrists
twist midnight swirls on
canvas pulled in every
direction, exhausted
in your craft for bleary
eyes to scrutinize, exhaust
universal meaning under
bright fluorescent lights

they mounted you boldly
on a bland wall, a clean
slate from your suicidal
tendencies, you bare
your soul while the
whole world watches

do you ever wish we'd
leave you alone?

you're exposed, naked, it
chills my shivering nerves
they call it your biting
bits of blue, your true
self set free with flicks of
yellow, an ounce of

brightness to mend your
broken bones, but i wonder

did you swallow enough of that
moonlight hue to make it
through the night?

[never good enough]

I always tell myself to write
more poetry I used to craft
such great melodies of you
between the
pages but once my pen hits
paper my brain falls
to the floor before you
stomp
stomp
stomp
on slippery memories
as a reminder that

you'll never be good enough
for me

[why?]

when I asked you "why
does it have to be like this" what
I meant was
"why do you have to be like all
the others who have long since
past?"

a living death

cathedral

i lost my grip on faith years past asleep
alone under the altar of my God's
cathedral. stain glass windows smashed
in another explosion of His wrath. i still
pull bloody shards out of my palms from
every time

I used to pray i could pick up His pieces

hallelujah and oxen free, come out come
out wherever you are, my god my God
why the fuck have you abandoned me?
i found my shot at sweet salvation
by writing down the past seven years
of my life through metaphors based
on a religion i can no longer trust

a god i lost from an early age when
i realized he will never be Upstairs
for me and the God I found between
dirty sheets and shared cigarette
drags during the early hours of a
warm summer Sunday

i overkill the Catholic imagery,
i spent half my life brainwashed
to believe that a baby can be born of a virgin
holy man and wholly god, i can't help myself
to think of these myths when my God,
an average man construed an idol for
crowds of cowering sheep, complicit in his
adultery, my God convinced himself that

he was Holy

i followed in His footsteps

cornered into sacrilege while he
conditioned me to breathe blind faith
in His likeness in hopes of being
saved. i bowed before my God
in penance, face crushed beneath
the feet i kissed as He delivered
His absolution
"I'm so sorry, I'm so so sorry baby
but it's not my goddamn fault"

i whispered hallelujah on hands
and knees, the shattered stained glass
digging deep into my hand's heartline
exposed on cold marble floor, I prayed
in silence that He might stop

"you've been a very bad girl" He cooed
into my neck as He cradled me within
His angry hands and held me over
three flights of stairs "show me that
you love me, only me"

how dare i love another god before Him!

for forty days and endless nights
i let myself grow far too cold on His
cathedral floor and wept for the day
He might return. "maybe if i were carved
from His side and crafted in His image maybe
then would He see that I am trying" but i
was far from perfect in His eyes and
i had failed Him.

my God is never to return again

so much time has passed since I started
praying i made this battered house my
home. it's far from perfect, foundation
built upon His broken image of me, a

sinner exiled from His promise
land, i am no longer cast within perpetual
light. only shadows shine down upon
my soul, spent and stretched thin
though I stumble blindly, hands outstretched
in the dark, i now see myself without
His grace

over time i carved offerings and profanity
for Him, for me, in the wood of worn down
pews, sang hosanna to the highest til my
throat became sore. I burned the Pascal
candle down to waxy remains months since
past just to show Him i could still seek light

hallelujah and oxen free, o my God,
show me Your divine mercy, i am heartily
sorry for having offended You, I'm
so so sorry, please please forgive me
i never thought i would make peace with
the pain He nailed deep in my chest but
i learned to carry this cross from the bottom
up i will swallow my pride hard and fast

before He could ever come
back to me

(He won't come back He never will)

it took me a lifetime but i found myself
buried under the rubble in the broken
home He left me. though i shake i learned
how to stand straight again and scream
into the rafters of this wholly holy
hallowed ground:

hallelujah and oxen free; it's been
fifteen months since my last confession
and these are my sins

buried deep on bloody hands, there
still remains this piece of glass i refuse
to pull out, though i have plucked in
patience and penance every shard to
wash my hands clean. through delusions
of faith and illusions of salvation my God once
promised me, i keep finding my finger
picking at the jagged edge of this
stubborn sliver, bleeding hot and sticky
over my knuckles with each little nudge.

scars from the others have yet to fade
but blood hasn't seeped through those
wounds since i chose to keep them exposed
and He no longer resides in me.

my time has come to repent and sin no more

[the difference between want and control]

i'm learning the difference
between wanting your hands
around my neck and craving
a razor blade pressed to my
thigh: it's all in the wrist and
my own control over who gets
to tell me when I break

bitch

you've screamed it a
thousand times. it's on
my clothes and in my
hair, carving deep
highways on my wrists
hoping each path will
send me straight to hell.

warm water won't scrub
me safe. it bleeds through
the spout in lethal doses of
plinks and *plops* until i'm
drowning in the kitchen
sink wondering what
happens if i swirl down
the drain. i only want erasure

if home is where the
heart is. I guess I'm left for
dead. swollen finger tips
still digging out
seven years' worth of grime
lodged in my bones while
bottled up fear sleeps
restlessly in my gut and my
head keeps spinning under
the anxiety of trying to
schedule a convenient time

to die. i want my body
bag shouting *dead on
arrival* in sharp tones and
shattered moans when they
find me. i'll be your blue

belief but you better be
damn sure to tell them
the bitch had it coming

respeak thunder

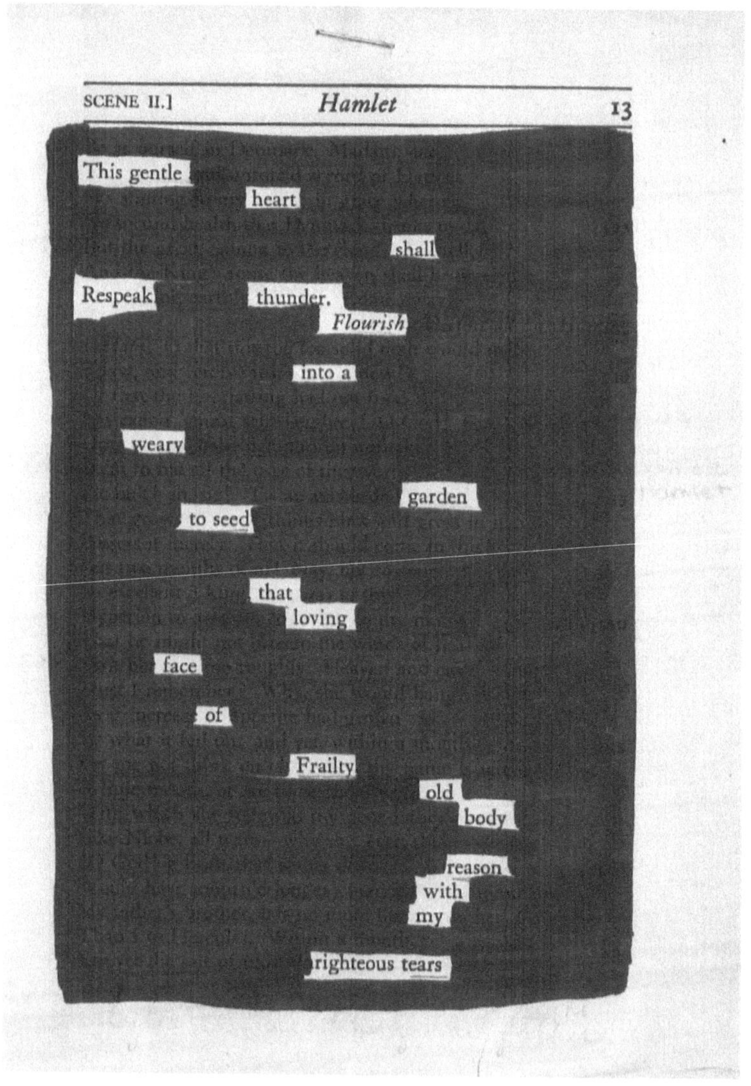

[ghost stories]

when someone asks me to talk
about you and me and when
you left me I can only recite
ghost stories filled with
labored groans and tortured
souls in the haunted house
you know I only wanted to call
home.

[a warning]

I hope you think of me
when you see your new
tattoo, the maddened
depression you locked
inside your cage taunting
me with the key lodged
between your teeth from
the first moment you
kissed me your canary
calls out in danger
deep within the mines
and suffocates from
the poison you put me
through so you could
make it out in the nick
of time I molt out of
season and stress and
struggle to figure out how
to claw my way through
this hell with battered
wings and broken bones

I hope you think of me,
between inked lines and
smothered cries and heed
your warning well

Babies, God damn it, you've got to be kind*

Your mother asked you to
write a different kind of
poem. "Not that depressing
crap. *Oh! Woe is me!*"

A happy poem.

About happy things.

Like fresh born babies, mere
seconds of life breathed out
of their tiny lungs. Newborn
eyes shut tight from the big
bad world they've been
forced out into. Or even
the older ones, the 6 monthers
starting to see sights for the first
time, tiny hands outstretched,
palms grasping at everything and
nothing, searching for answers
in smiles and coos and Mama's
hair. Little 18 month olds
sprawled out on the carpet, feet
failing to lead them but
perseverance, nevertheless. All
these months of life, little one, and
you still don't know your age.

Happy things.

For a happy poem.

But damn, that's hard when you're
on the cusp of 288 months
old and you haven't had a

happy memory since your
168th month birthday.

You have a lot of pain and
sorrow that can only be best
presented in a twisted pattern
of poetic word play and suicidal
ideation of a well placed bullet
point list of harsh enjambment.

It's not your fault you've
crafted somber nursery
rhymes to lull you to sleep
when Mom stopped singing
the cheerful ones to you.

But you know what?
You're only 272 months
old, exactly 2 Point 5 in
dog years (and it took you
that long to discover that
dogs age 10.5 years faster
than their whiny infant
owners, always crying for
no reason, because we're
hungry, because we're
sitting in diapers, so full
of shit).

Little one, you're just a baby, you
shouldn't be so sad. You have no
taxes and bills and doctor
appointments and childhood
trauma and former abusers
to deal with every day. By God!
it's a miracle you've been potty
trained! The struggle of life
would leave the sanest baby
shitting their pants well after

22 months old. Goddamn, look
out world, you're growing up.

So you wrote this poem
because she wanted happy
when she only gave you
years (or whichever unit you
prefer) of sad. In fact,
this poem was supposed to be
an ode to happy things, or at
least the happy things you've
know are out there just to
make you feel less sad

but

in your 10.5 old dog age, you've
forgotten those lines (I guess
you can't teach an old dog
new tricks). Where did the
happy go before your eyes
shut back tight against it all?
Little one, your 324 month
birthday has come and past,
the clock a ticking time
bomb beating back against
every breath you've tried to
call your last.

There should be happy
somewhere in that infant
mind of yours, but the lines
sour on the page when all
you've got is sad and pain
and pills and too many months
and years of pent up rage and
existential dread best told
with waving hands

swaying bodies

jabbing

stabbing

lagging

dragging

swerving

punchy rhythms found deep
in slam poems (which, despite
common misconception, is not
when you throw your pen on the
ground, unless that pen still writes
the words you scream into
silent spaces on violent nights).

This is the best you've got.
It's not much, but it'll do.

At least this isn't as depressing
as the last time you ended something
you wrote with:

I'm sorry I disappointed you, Mom.

*Title from Kurt Vonnegut's novel *God Bless You, Mr. Rosewater* (1965). In the poet's 1991 edition of Vonnegut's classic, it can be found on page 93, published through Laurel in 1991 and Dell Publishing in 1965.

Vonnegut, Kurt. *God Bless You, Mr. Rosewater or Pearls before Swine.* Laurel, 1991.

a phantom memory

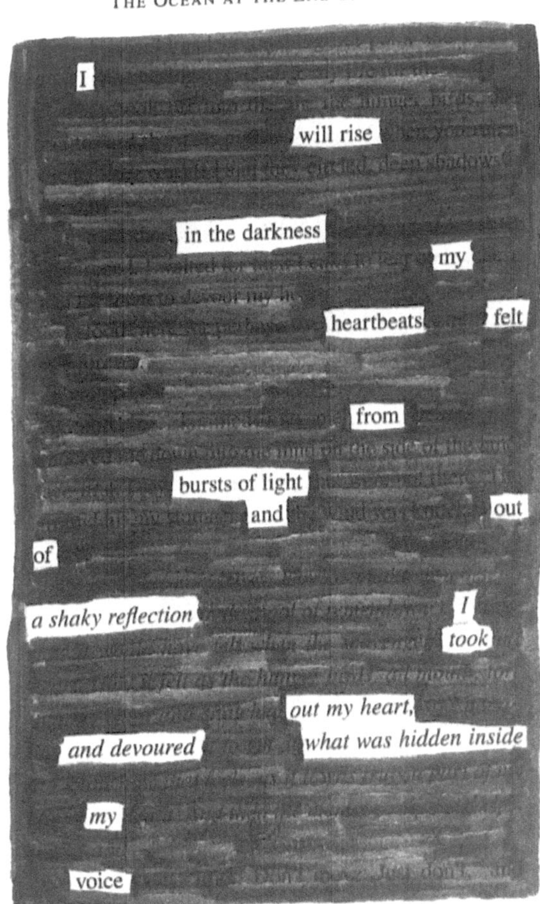

[red glass]

my jacket smells like red glass
shards and whispered lies lost
between cracks on hardwood
floors. gentle lips pull bloody
slivers from my palm. seal me

with a
broken
kiss

you watched me shatter under a
cautious touch, too frail to grasp
your hands in mine. we sought
out the dark with anxious hearts
my fragments freezing in the

cold
let
me

shiver in the autumn night with
fabricated truth slung around my
shaking frame. clasp me tight
inside your shaky hands. i wear

my
nervous
heart

on my sleeve and
scattered on my wrists, clattered
with your soul stretched out on
black leather tossed against your
cigarette stain couch. sear another
ill-placed flame in my faded arm

rest
press
me

hard into your body, hold me
close, weigh me down. piece
my bones together beneath your
sheets with careful calloused
hands. bruises

make
me
whole

i wrote a poem about this
once, but the meaning wasn't true.
this scent now lingers in my skin
and i know you know poetry will

heighten me
to all your
senses

In regards to the political events on October 6, 2018

I am with you, Dr. Ford,
as he forced your walls of comfort
down into unfamiliar sheets
the beer beating on his breath
louder than the music made to
muffle your sobs

I am with you, Dr. Ford,
sticky with a summer sweat caked
in chlorine and a cry for help
his fingers pushing back your second
skin in a drunken stupor you didn't
ask for

I am with you, Dr. Ford,
as he crushes your bones between
his hands like his fifth beer can
sloshed down past his lips and
over his shirt

I am with you, Dr. Ford,
when he takes what little sobriety he
has left to realize he's hurting you and
no one has to know palms coated

in pabst

(his prized possession on the first floor and
the only blue ribbon he ever snatched at summer camp)

pressed so harsh against your
screams you thought his whole fist
might shatter your teeth and slam
against the back of your throat

you thought he might kill you

And though I was not in that room
with you, Dr. Ford, I feel that fear far
too well. I taste it when accidents
happen and suddenly the blood from
an over chewed lip goes down like the
night I thought I'd bite my whole
mouth off, the pain, his weight, the
inebriation hanged heavy in the
bedroom between hits off his pipe.

When the party ended and I
scrambled to collect my clothes with
myself after insisting tonight wasn't
right

I feel sick

I've got a headache

I'm tired.

I'm so fucking tired.

Dr. Ford, I'm tired of men who cower
like boys when we finally get to tell
them no. I'm tired of men hysterical,
naked, howling for their angry power
fix. I am tired of writing poems about
it to get the ghost of his force off my
wrists, hips, thighs, face, throat if
only between lines and forced
enjambment

He may have won, and Dr. Ford, I
know that pain the most but our

battle never ends as we force
ourselves back into the functions of
every day life after death of our
innocence and what once was before
we quivered at the altar of malicious
men, hands on our heart and over the
only thing, living or dead, left sacred
in this world we live in. We survive,
Dr. Ford, we rise out of the darkness
where we once laid, as greedy
bodies marked us a fraternity pledge

Allegiance to the flag of the United
States of America. And to the
Republic for which it stands, one
Nation, under g_d, indivisible with
_________ and _________ for _________.

[uprising]

you killed two birds with one
stone just to see how each
would die: the first, my body
 a city pigeon begging for the
scraps of what little breadcrumb
love you had to offer me; my
firebird heart your second prey
with plumage for profit when
Narcissus blossoms

you missed the phoenix inside
my heart whose love for you
sparked flames upon each feathered
wing, but crumbled to ashes when
you doused the wild fire

while your stone lodged straight
into my skull like a
suicidal bullet. my heart beats
strong: the phoenix reborn

NO VACANCY

I will not write another
poem about you.

I will not let you dwell
inside my head, your likeness
embedded in my brain, your name
carved sharp with your trusty pocket
knife on the prefrontal cortex like that
time you etched *forever* into your arm
chair when I asked you how long we'd
be together. You needed a new couch
anyways and you weren't afraid to toss
me to the curb alongside it, longing
for something new, something whole,
something you hadn't damaged yet,
but I let you stay, much longer than
I should have, even after all I've
come to understand about you.

I let you stay on borrowed time,
my poems the void you stole
from me, my voice taken from
the present tense, thoughts bridged
between the *is* and *was* you've
built around me. I don't feel safe

inside my head.

Thoughts looming on the cusp
of *now* and *then,* my self-control
a cat's cradle weaved in your
hands, fingers pulling every
thread tight against my throat

You smother me.

And every time I bash my head
into the wall to get *you* out of
my words, or choose to burn
a line you crossed, you sink
further into the wreck you've
made out of the black-and-
white grey matter, praying for
one bad storm to dig you out.
You can't stay
here anymore.

No, you will no longer take residency
in my hippocampus with your finger
on the trigger sounding all the alarms
at any time *you* please, and not when
I need them most. But when I've
finally forgotten your presence and
life looks good for one clear moment,

the threat of you

digs up every memory I buried, every fire
I doused, as you smolder in the ashes
of your smoke and mirror show.

(It was a pleasure to burn
you over and over again)

I will not allow you here as summer's
heat blurs the edges between *now* and
then and I can't tell if my back aches
from my weight giving in to this ancient
mattress or your hands pressed into my
spine, forcing *there* to buckle around
me when *here* is where I am and
here is where I should be and *everything's
fine now, I got you this time.* My eyes
won't fixate in the dark, your ghost
still saturates the shadow truths of

what was and *what should have
never happened.* You thrive best
at night when light and time can't
catch you in the act still rolling out
your greatest hits and my bleakest
days over and over again.

You can't stay
here anymore.

Inside my mind.
Behind my eyes.
Under my skin.
Around my neck.

Living and breathing
in a space that would
no longer need warning
shots fired into the back
of my head if you just
left it in the first place.

You smother me.

And I will not write another
poem about you.

I simply have too much of
everything else to think about,
too many new things begging for
the flicker of the vacancy sign
inside my head, a neon red
herring to future inhabitants. This
home now comes with a liability
waver, utilities not included. I'm
not renting this space to just
anyone these days, and I most
certainly will not let you live here
any longer.

(I should have never saved
the uppercase for you)

Because when you said you'd stay
forever, I didn't think your
voice would echo in the empty
hollow behind my eardrums,
haunting whispers swollen in
every inch of space you can
latch on to, and no matter how
hard I've been searching I can
never seem to find the nearest exit.

Things have changed,
whether you're still here or not

You're nothing more than a fool in
King's clothing, a residual haunt
inside a foreclosed home. I've dug
a grave for you in memory of *what
was* and *what will never be again.*

Let your bones rot inside your
shallow hell, you're not going
anywhere beyond these pages.

Perpetual Thunder
Storm Destruction

there's a thunderstorm inside my
attic, cumulonimbus clouds billow
and bloat in the rafters, bolts of
lightning strike wooden beams,
torrential showers soaked through
my insulation. the tornado in the
basement bashes back and forth
between brick walls and beckons a
break in the infrastructure seams.

i have been without power
for one thousand and ninety-five
days, give or take. my eyes finally
accumulated to the dark. i only see in
present tense and often long to remember
the squint and crinkle in my face on a
sunny summer day. thunder tosses and
tumbles me up at night and i haven't
figured out if it's a cold sweat or the
constant drip of my leaky ceiling
that swims between brow and hairline.

i've lost shelter to the twister i'm too
afraid to tackle. it streamlines straight
and narrow and i can't even open the
cellar door, the shrill of a derailed train
shrieks and shakes on every floor, the
havoc eager to swallow me whole.

i have never been much of a storm chaser.

so i deal.

no power
no safety

only sandbags half full and flood walls
hoisted high around my bedposts.

i asked my local meteorologists to
categorize this unnatural string of
natural phenomena. the diagnosis:

Cumulus Congestus
or

(in layman's terms)

Perpetual Thunder Storm Destruction.
"More common than you'd think." from
which one in nine upstanding citizens such
as myself suffer. they say they can't
pinpoint predictions on these weather
patterns, but warnings are issued when
conditions cumulate after severe
circumstances. households plagued by
these storms should seek comfort in sheets
of rain and fifteen to thirty seconds
between each rolling wave of thunder.

so i deal.

the power's projected to come back
in due time. till then i've sheathed
the bedside lamp with an umbrella
and wait for the clouds to break

and the drizzle to simmer
and the bulb to flicker and glow.

About Atmosphere Press

Atmosphere Press is an independent, full-service publisher for excellent books in all genres and for all audiences. Learn more about what we do at atmosphere-press.com.

We encourage you to check out some of Atmosphere's latest releases, which are available at Amazon.com and via order from your local bookstore:

In the Cloakroom of Proper Musings, a lyric narrative by Kristina Moriconi

Lucid_Malware.zip, poetry by Dylan Sonderman

The Unordering of Days, poetry by Jessica Palmer

It's Not About You, poetry by Daniel Casey

A Dream of Wide Water, poetry by Sharon Whitehill

Radical Dances of the Ferocious Kind, poetry by Tina Tru

The Woods Hold Us, poetry by Makani Speier-Brito

My Cemetery Friends: A Garden of Encounters at Mount Saint Mary in Queens, New York, nonfiction and poetry by Vincent J. Tomeo

Report from the Sea of Moisture, poetry by Stuart Jay Silverman

The Enemy of Everything, poetry by Michael Jones

The Stargazers, poetry by James McKee

About the Author

V. Rendina is a poet and writer from Northeastern Pennsylvania. She more commonly goes by her full name, but enjoys the mystique of the initial. Her work has been published in Wilkes University's literary magazine, *The Manuscript,* and has circulated among 38 buses in her home county as part of the *Poetry in Transit* program in 2016. She collects old editions of her favorite books and reads Neil Gaiman in her spare time. This is her first publication.